Assessment of Estuarine Water and Sediment Quality at Canaveral National Seashore, 2009

Natural Resource Data Series NPS/SECN/NRDS—2011/283

M. Brian Gregory

National Park Service
Southeast Coast Inventory and Monitoring Network
160 Phoenix Road
Athens, GA 30605

Katy Austin Smith

University of Georgia
Marine Extension Service
715 Bay Street
Brunswick, GA 31520

January 2011

U.S. Department of the Interior
National Park Service
Natural Resource Program Center
Fort Collins, Colorado

The National Park Service, Natural Resource Program Center publishes a range of reports that address natural resource topics of interest and applicability to a broad audience in the National Park Service and others in natural resource management, including scientists, conservation and environmental constituencies, and the public.

The Natural Resource Data Series is intended for the timely release of basic data sets and data summaries. Care has been taken to assure accuracy of raw data values, but a thorough analysis and interpretation of the data has not been completed. Consequently, the initial analyses of data in this report are provisional and subject to change.

All manuscripts in the series receive the appropriate level of peer review to ensure that the information is scientifically credible, technically accurate, appropriately written for the intended audience, and designed and published in a professional manner.

Data in this report were collected and analyzed using methods based on established, peer-reviewed protocols and were analyzed and interpreted within the guidelines of the protocols.

Views, statements, findings, conclusions, recommendations, and data in this report do not necessarily reflect views and policies of the National Park Service, U.S. Department of the Interior. Mention of trade names or commercial products does not constitute endorsement or recommendation for use by the U.S. Government.

This report is available from the Southeast Coast Network (http://science.nature.nps.gov/im/units/secn) and the Natural Resource Publications Management website (http://www.nature.nps.gov/publications/nrpm)

Please cite this publication as:

Gregory, M. Brian, and K. A. Smith. 2011. Assessment of estuarine water and sediment quality at Canaveral National Seashore, 2009. Natural Resource Report NPS/SECN/NRR—2011/283. National Park Service, Fort Collins, Colorado.

NPS 639/106363, January 2011

Contents

Summary and Key Findings

1. In July 2009, the Southeast Coast Network and the University of Georgia conducted an assessment of water and sediment quality at Canaveral National Seashore (CANA) as a part of the NPS Vital Signs Monitoring Program.

2. Monitoring was conducted following methods developed by the U.S. Environmental Protection Agency as a part of the National Coastal Assessment Program and included laboratory analysis for chlorophyll a, total dissolved nitrogen and phosphorous concentrations and field measurements of water temperature, pH, dissolved oxygen, and salinity. Estimates of water clarity were made using secchi depth measurements and were adjusted for naturally occurring water-clarity conditions.

3. Overall water quality at the park ranged from *Fair* to *Poor* with the majority of sites found to be in *Fair* condition (93 percent).

4. Nitrogen levels were at concentrations considered to be *Poor* at 90 percent of the sites sampled. These consistently high levels indicate potential nonpoint sources of pollution in the watershed as well as an overall phosphorus limited system. Only one site was observed with concentrations of both nitrogen and phosphorus considered to be *Poor*.

5. Three sites at Canaveral had two or more *Poor* water quality ratings — CANA-12 and CANA 27 which had *Poor* water clarity and elevated nitrogen levels and CANA-25 which had elevated nitrogen and phosphorus levels.

6. Overall sediment conditions were considered *Good* at all sites sampled showing only traces amounts of metal contamination and little or no organic contamination. Relatively clean sediments at Canaveral National Seashore are potentially due to the high levels of sand and low levels of total organic carbon in the benthic sediments reducing its ability to bind contaminants.

7. Aside from the generally high levels of nitrogen found across the park no distinctive spatial patterns in the data suggested areas of immediate concern. Continued monitoring of nutrients might help detect problems in the future and might be prudent due to the level of development upstream of the park's boundaries.

Intro luction

Estuarie s are semi-e closed coastal bodies of water that have free c onnection with the open sea and within which se i water mixes with fresh water. A k ey defining feature of an estuary is that it is an int rface between sea water and fresh water and th ere is an influence of the ocean tide creating a dynamic relationship between the two waters. Estuaries c ontain critical habitat for a variety of fish and wildlife species. They serve as nursery habitats f or fish, crustaceans, and shellfish and foraging habitat for birds and mammals w ile providing a multitude of recreational opportu ities including boating, fishing, and bird watching. These a e fragile ecosystems vulnerable to impacts caused by development and many other uses. Severe impacts including alteratio is to hydrodynamic processes, exposure to levels of chemical contaminants that cause mortalit , altered gr wth, and reduced reproduction and exposure to more frequent and severe hypoxia have been s hown in estuarine habitats due to ur ban and ind istrial development (Lerberg et al. 20)0). Although some nutrient inputs to coastal w ters are nat ral and necessary for a healthy, functioning estuarine ecosystem. When nutrients from vari ous sources, such as sewage and ferti lizers, are introduced into an estuary, the conce itration of available nutrients will increase beyond nat iral background levels. This increas e in the rate of supply of organic matter is called eutrophicat on, which may result in a host of undesirable water-quality conditions. Excess nutrients can lead to excess plant production, an l thus, to in reased chlorophyll, which can decr ase water clarity and lower concentrations of dissolved oxygen. In addition, macrobenthic communities in impacted areas are often characterize l by low diversity, low numbers of rare and pollution sensitive species, and low abundance (Lerberg et al. 2000). In areas wi h increased impervious cover, stormwater runo ff is flashier and occurs in greater volumes than in und veloped areas. This unnatural runoff can often be polluted with a wide variety of low-level contaminants that are released into estuaries an l can accumulate in sediment (Hollan et al. 2004).

A wide variety of metals and organic substances, such as polycycli aromatic hydrocarbons (PAHs), polychlorinated biphen ls (PCBs), nd pesticides, are disch rged into estuaries from urban, agricultural, and industrial sources in the watershed. The contaminants a lsorb onto suspend d particles ind eventually accumulate in depositional basins where they can disrupt the benthic community of invert brates, shellfish, and crus aceans that live in or on the sediments. To the xtent that t ie contami iants become concentrated in the organisms, they pose a risk to organis is throughо it the food web—including humans.

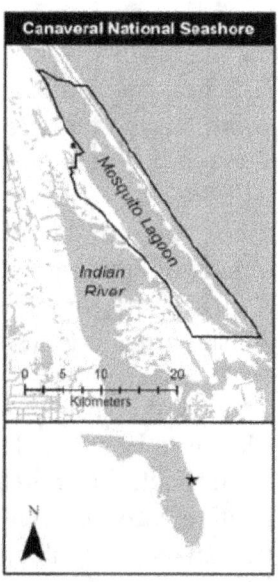

Several actors influ nce the extent and severity of contamination. Fine-grained, organic-ric sediments are likely to become resuspended a id transpor ed to distant locations and are also efficient at scavenging pollutan s. Thus, silty sediments high in total organic ca bon (TOC) are potential sources of contamination. Conversely, organic-rich particl s bind so e toxicants so strongly that the threat to organi ms can be greatly r duced.

of
il
a.

Natural esources at Canaveral National Seashore (Figure 1) include a diverse ssemblage f wildlife, plant communities, geophysical feat res

---

and natural processes reflecting the complexity of the land/lagoon/sea interface of east central Florida. Throughout the park, the relationship of land and water is paramount. Unlike many barrier islands, Canaveral National Seashore has only a single dune ridge, averaging 12 feet in height. For the vast majority of its length the dune is quite stable, backed by a dense growth of saw palmetto (*Serenoa repens*) and several other species of hardy shrubs and grasses. Mosquito Lagoon, extending along the backside of Canaveral National Seashore's barrier island, is the northernmost part of the Indian River Lagoon. Containing the most diverse assemblage of aquatic species on the entire eastern seaboard, this 155-mile long lagoon has been designated as an Estuary of National Significance by the Environmental Protection Agency and an Outstanding Florida Water by the State of Florida. It contains one of the last significant populations of oysters on the entire Atlantic Coast that has not been depleted by over harvesting or pollution. Commercial shell fishing is extremely important to the local economy; recreational fishing and shrimping in the lagoon support a multimillion-dollar tourist industry. The estuary also acts as an important nursery area for a number of commercially important ocean-going species such as flounder, mullet, black drum and shrimp.

Wildlife resources are considerable, ranging from myriad terrestrial and aquatic species inhabiting estuarine systems to small endemic populations of mammals living in the dunes. Canaveral National Seashore is second only to Everglades National Park in number of federally protected species with 14. These include such species as the highly endangered West Indian manatee (*Trichechus manatus*), right whale (*Balaena glacialis*) and little known Atlantic salt marsh snake (*Nerodia fasciata taeniata*), who's entire known range consists of a single county in Florida. Canaveral's 24 miles of beach provides a critical nesting area for sea turtles, harboring 3,000 to 4,000 nests each year. The majority are loggerhead (*Caretta caretta*), with a smaller number of green (*Chelonia mydas*) and an occasional leatherback (*Dermochelys coriacea*). Mosquito Lagoon provides an important nursery area for juvenile sea turtles.

Boaters are coming into Canaveral National Seashore in increasing numbers due to the growing popularity of fly-fishing for redfish. This increases the destruction of seagrass beds, impacts to fisheries are unknown and manatees are highly affected. One of the very controversial and volatile issues among boaters in Florida is the establishment of slow speed zones to protect the West Indian manatee. Canaveral has supplied sighting data and engaged in several discussions with Florida Department of Environmental Protection (FDEP) on the proper placement of slow speed zones in the vicinity of the park. Additionally, the park has long been concerned about the impact of commercial harvesting on hard clams (*Mercenaria* spp.) and eastern oysters (*Crassostrea virginica*). As shellfish have been depleted along other portions of the Atlantic coast, harvesting pressure has increased significantly in Mosquito Lagoon.

Canaveral National Seashore faces a number of complex issues regarding water quality in Mosquito Lagoon. These include septic tank, agricultural and industrial effluents, mosquito control activities, dredging of the Intracoastal Waterway, impacts of aquaculture, and increased boating activity. While water quality in Mosquito Lagoon has been reported as quite good overall, septic tank effluent and stormwater runoff from adjacent communities may pose threats to the lagoon system. Currently park waters are closed to shell fishing when rainfall exceeds 1.5 inches in a 72-hour period, due to high fecal coliform levels. Another of the delicate issues with which Canaveral National Seashore must grapple is mosquito control. In the designation of lands for NPS management, both NASA and the State of Florida stipulated that Canaveral

National Seashore must cooperate with the local mosquito control districts to control salt marsh mosquitoes. Canaveral National Seashore and East Volusia Mosquito Control District have tested several measures to reduce the use of chemicals and to restore lost salt marsh.

In July 2009, the Southeast Coast Network Inventory and Monitoring Program in cooperation with the University of Georgia conducted an assessment of water and sediment quality at Canaveral National Seashore as a part of the Network's Vital Signs Monitoring program (DeVivo et al., 2008). The purpose of this document is to report the most recently collected data from within the park as part of an ongoing long-term water-quality monitoring program. This report has been designed to provide the water-quality monitoring data to managers in a concise summary format in the context of applicable Federal Standards that were developed by the U.S. EPA. Other data collected during this survey are available at (http://www.nature.nps.gov/publications/NRPM).

Meth ds

Water-q ality assessment was conducted in estuarine and tidal cree : waters following the methods developed ϸy the Environmental Protection Agency's Nati ϸnal Coastal Assessment Program (U.S. EPA, 2001). Descriptions of the water-quality para ϸeters and the assessment criteria are from EP ϸ's National Coastal Assessment II Report (2005). Methods suggested for use in thϸse protocols were adapted in part and integrateϸ into protoϸols tailored specifically for parks in the Southeaϸt Coast Network (Devivo and others, *in review*). Site selection and sampling methodology are briϸfly outlined in the following sectioϸs.

Site Selection

Thirty sites within t e boundaries of Canaveral National Seashore ere randomly selected for monitoring followinϸ methods developed by the U.S. EPA (Stevens, 1997; Stevens and Olsen, 1999; Stϸvens and Olsen, 2004) (Figure 2). A pool of al ernate sites was also selected to use if any of t e original sites were not accessible. This method of randomly selecting sites in a spatially balanced manner provides managers with a statistically valid estimate of the overall conditioϸs of assessϸd resources within or around the park.

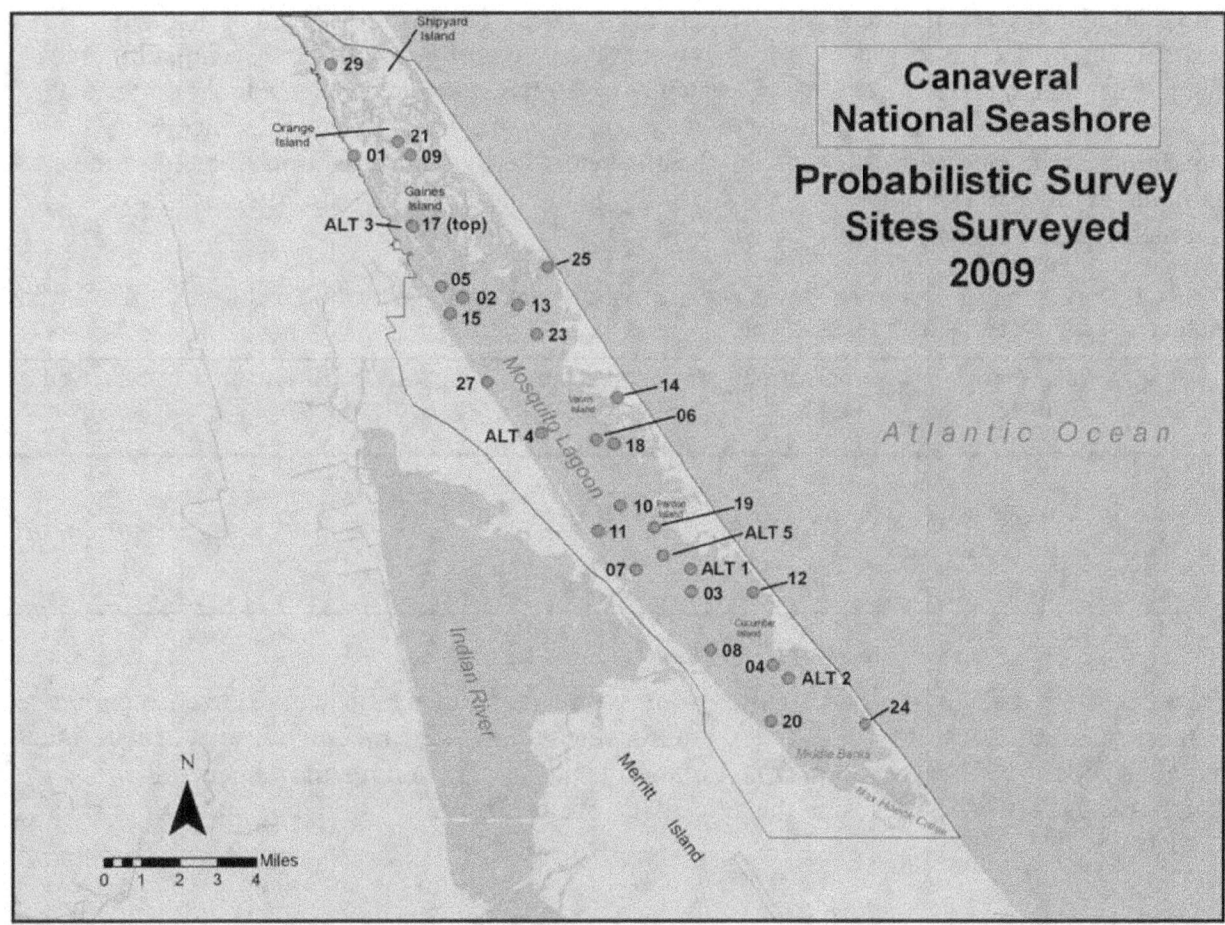

Figure 2. Location map showing sites sampled during July 2)09 at Canaveral National Seashore.

Water-Quality Data Collection

The water-quality assessment conducted during this survey period included conducting hydrographic profiles at from 0.5 to 1.0 m intervals at each site for temperature, pH, dissolved oxygen, and salinity. Concurrent measurements of chlorophyll a levels were made with nutrient samples at the surface, mid, and bottom depths, depending on total water depths, by filtering known volumes onto glass fiber filters. Filters and water samples were refrigerated and submitted for laboratory analysis. Shallow water sites (> than 1m) were assessed using only one surface sample. Estimates of water clarity were made at each site using a secchi disk to estimate light extinction depth which was converted to light attenuation coefficients corrected for naturally occurring turbidity conditions (Smith et al., 2006). Water clarity was not assessed at sites too shallow to ascertain an accurate secchi depth measurement. When sites were too shallow to access by boat, alternate sites were used.

Water-Quality Assessment Criteria

Water quality was assessed for each of the parameters following the East / Gulf Coast site criteria in EPA's National Coastal Assessment II Report (2005). The categorical assessments (i.e., *good, fair, and poor*) use measurements of chlorophyll a, nutrients, dissolved oxygen and water clarity (Table 1) and are intended to characterize acutely degraded water-quality conditions and does not consistently identify sites experiencing occasional or infrequent hypoxia, nutrient enrichment, or decreased water clarity. As a result, a rating of *poor* for the water-quality index means that the site is likely to have consistently exhibited *poor* conditions before or after the assessment period. If a site is designated as *fair* or *good*, the site did not experience *poor* condition on the date sampled, but could be characterized by *poor* conditions for short time periods. In order to assess the level of variability in the index at a specific site, increased or supplemental sampling would be needed.

Table 1. Condition criteria applied to water-quality parameters collected by the Southeast Coast Network during Coastal Water Quality assessment.

Rating	Water Clarity Index (WCI)	Chlorophyll a (ug/L)	Total Dissolved Nitrogen (mg/L)	Total Dissolved Phosphorus (mg/L)	Dissolved Oxygen (mg/L)
Good	<2.3	< 5	< 0.1	< 0.01	> 5
Fair	2.3 – 2.99	5 – 20	0.1 – 0.5	0.01 – 0.05	2 – 5
Poor	> 3.00	> 20	> 0.5	> 0.05	< 2
Missing					

Assessments were also be made by using an index that combines ratings given to each parameter into a site-specific Water-Quality Index Rating which allows general comparisons between sites within a park as well as overall park conditions (Table 2). This rating allows general comparisons between parks using the percentage of sites that fall within the good, fair or poor categories.

Table 2. Condition criteria used for water-quality assessment summaries at individual sampling sites and park.

Rating	Site Water Quality Index Rating	Park Water Quality Index Rating
Good	A maximum of one indicator is fair, and no indicators are poor.	Less than 10% of sites are in poor condition and less than 50% of sites are in combined poor and fair condition.
Fair	One of the indicators is rated poor, or two or more indicators are rated fair.	10% to 20% of sites are in poor condition, or more than 50% of sites are in combined fair and poor condition
Poor	Two or more of the five indicators are rated poor.	More than 20% of sites are in poor condition
Missing	Two components of the indicator are missing and the available indicators do not suggest a fair or poor rating	

Sediment Data Collection

Assessments of sediment quality are used to indicate the potential for sediment contaminants to affect bottom-dwelling organisms. Sediments sample were collected by taking multiple grabs at each site using a Van Veen sampler. The top 2-3 cm from each sample were composited and split in to three separate samples that were analyzed for organic contaminants, metals, total organic carbon (TOC), and grain size.

Due to missing TOC data at four sites which would have prevented the calculation of the overall sediment-quality rating, TOC level were estimated based on the significant correlation ($r = -0.76$) between percent sands and TOC concentration established at the other sampled sites within the park using a linear function shown in Figure 3 ($y = -12.54 x + 1612.1$, $R^2 = 0.58$). Sites using the estimated values to calculate the sediment quality index are identified in Table 7.

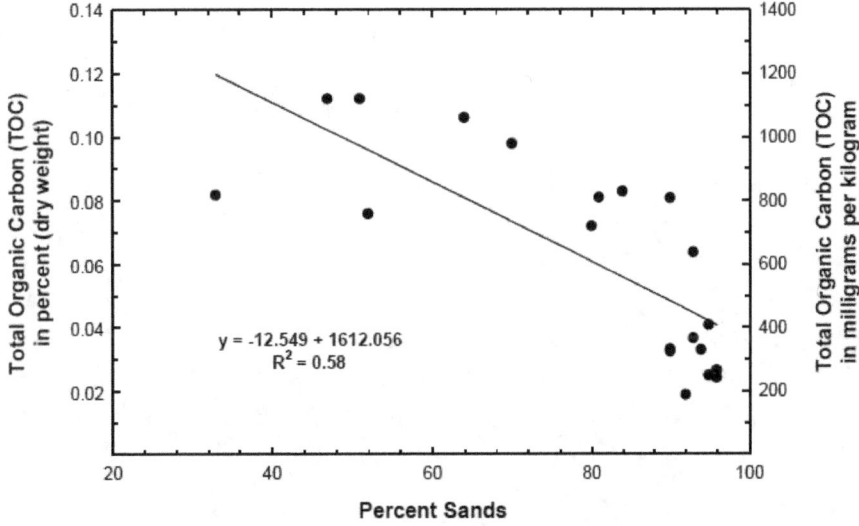

Figure 3. Relation between total organic carbon (TOC) concentration and percent sand in benthic sediment samples at Canaveral National Seashore in July, 2009.

Sediment Assessment Criteria
There are no absolute chemical concentrations that correspond to sediment toxicity, but Effects Range Low (ERL) and Effects Range Median (ERM) values are used as guidelines in assessing sediment contamination (Table 3; Long et al., 1995). ERM is the median concentration of a contaminant observed to have adverse biological effects in the literature studies examined. A more protective indicator of contaminant concentration is the ERL criteria, which is the 10th percentile concentration of a contaminant represented by studies demonstrating adverse biological effects in the literature. Ecological effects are not likely to occur at contaminant concentrations below the ERL criterion. The criteria for rating sediment contaminants at individual sampling sites are shown in Table 4.

Sediment contaminant availability or organic enrichment can be altered in areas where there is considerable deposition of organic matter. Sediment toxicity from organic matter is assessed by measuring TOC. The criteria for rating TOC for individual sampling sites are shown in Table 4.

After sediment contaminants and sediment TOC were assessed for a given site, the sediment quality index rating was calculated for the site and park based on these three indicators. The sediment quality index was rated good to poor for each site using the criteria shown in Table 4.

Table 3. Sediment contaminant guidance values from Long et al. (1995). ERL (Effects Range Low) thresholds are determined for each chemical as the 10th percentile in a database of ascending concentrations associated with biological effects. ERM (Effects Range Median) thresholds are determined for each chemical as the 50th percentile (median) in a database of ascending concentrations associated with adverse biological effects.

Contaminant	ERL	ERM
Metals (ppm)[a]		
Arsenic	8.2	70
Cadmium	1.2	9.6
Chromium	81	370
Copper	37	270
Lead	46.7	218
Mercury	0.15	0.71
Nickel	20.9	51.6
Silver	1	3.7
Zinc	150	410
Organics (ppb)[b]		
Acenaphthene	16	500
Acenapthylene	44	640
Anthracene	85.3	1,100
Flourene	19	540
2-Methyl napthalene	70	670
Napthalene	160	2,100
Phenanthrene	240	1,500
Benz(a)anthracene	261	1,600
Benzo(a)pyrene	430	1,600
Chrysene	384	2,800
Dibenzo(a,h)anthracene	63.4	260
Fluoranthene	600	5,100
Pyrene	665	2,600
Low molecular weight PAH	552	3,160
High molecular weight PAH	1,700	9,600
Total PAHs	4,020	44,800
4,4'-DDE	2.2	27
Total DDT	1.6	46.1
Total PCBs	22.7	180

[a] Units are ug/g dry sediment, equivalent to ppm.
[b] Units are ng/g dry sediment, equivalent to ppb.

Table 4. Condition criteria for sediment contaminants.

Rating	Sediment Contaminants Rating (SC)	% Total Organic Carbon (TOC)	Site Sediment Quality Index (SQI)	Park Sediment Quality Index
Good	No ERM concentrations are exceeded and less than five ERL concentrations are exceeded.	< 2%	TOC is good and Sediment Contaminants Rating is good.	Less than 5% of the sites are rated in *Poor* condition and less than 50% of the sites are rated in combined *Poor* and *Fair* condition.
Fair	Five or more ERL concentrations are exceeded.	2% – 5%	TOC is fair or Sediment Contaminants Rating is fair.	5% to 15% of sites are in *Poor* condition, or more than 50% of sites are in combined *Poor* and *Fair* condition.
Poor	An ERM concentration is exceeded for one or more contaminants	> 5%	TOC is poor or Sediment Contaminants Indicator is poor.	More than 15% of sites are in *Poor* condition

Wate ·-Qualit / Condition Assessme ıts

Figures 1 through 8 show maps illustrating the spatial distribution o∵sampling sites and the corresponding ratings for water clarity, chlorophyll a, total dissolved nitrogen, total dissolved phosphorus, and dis olved oxygen based on each param eter's corresponding condition category. Figure 9 show water-quality conditions summary for the park. Data used to make maps and graphs a e in table 5.

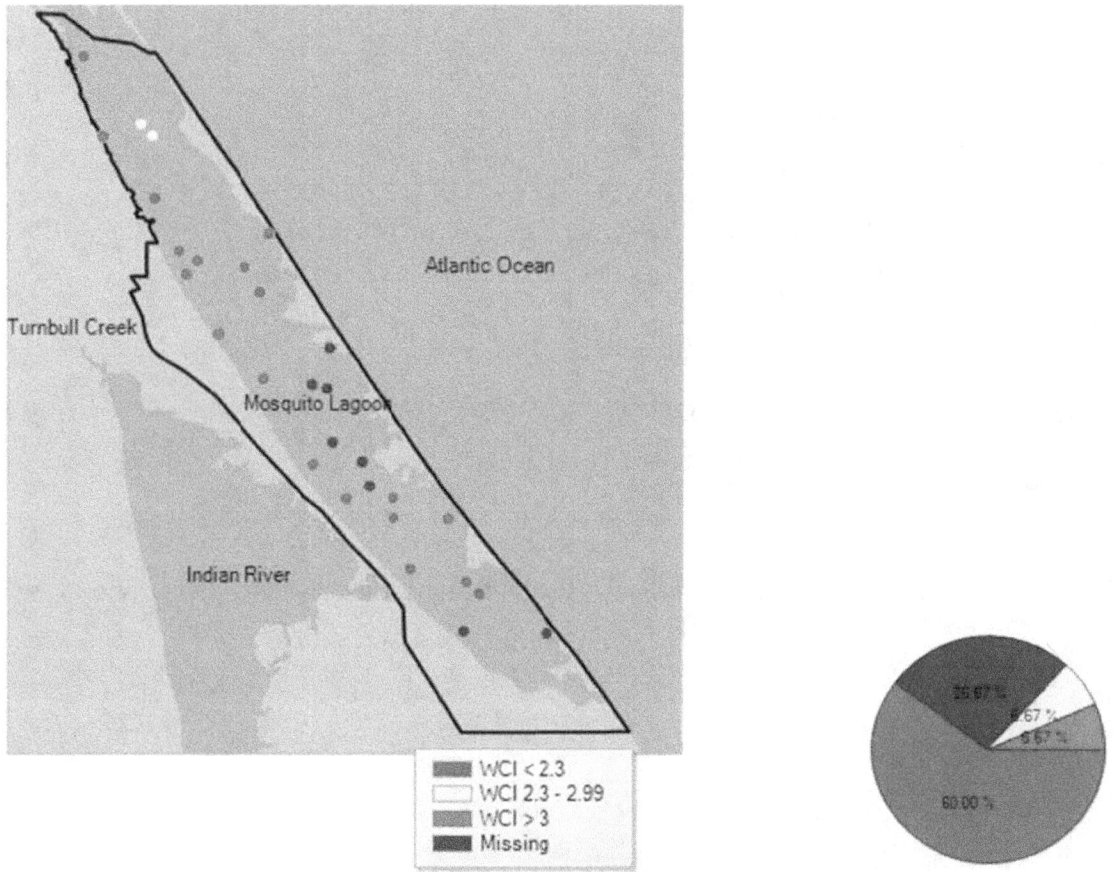

Figure 4. Water clarit index (*k*) based on light attenuation e timates at s mpling sites at Canaveral National Seashore during July 2009. Graph shows the perce tage of sites in each condition category. Missing data indicated places where the water clarity index c ould not be calculated due to limited water depth.

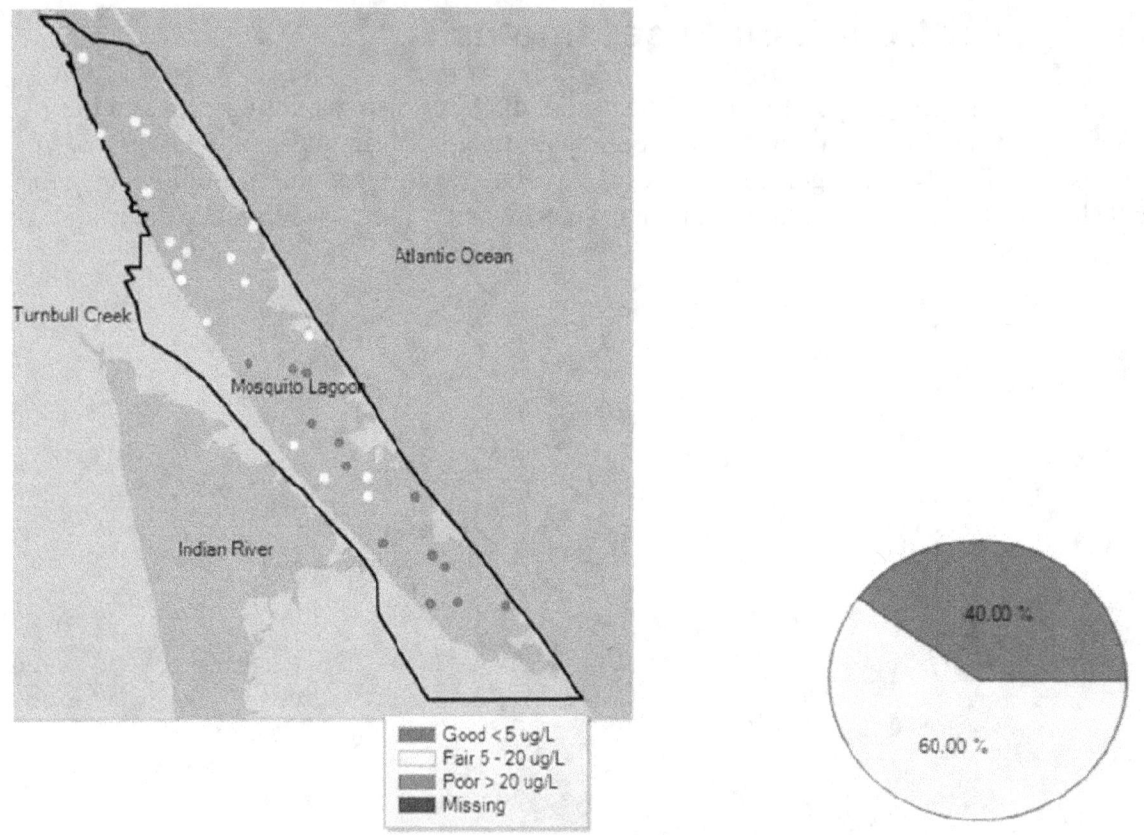

Good < 5 ug/L
Fair 5 - 20 ug/L
Poor > 20 ug/L
Missing

40.00 %

60.00 %

Figure 5. Chlorophyll a concentrations at Canaveral National Seashore in July 2009. Graph shows the percenta је of sites in each condition category.

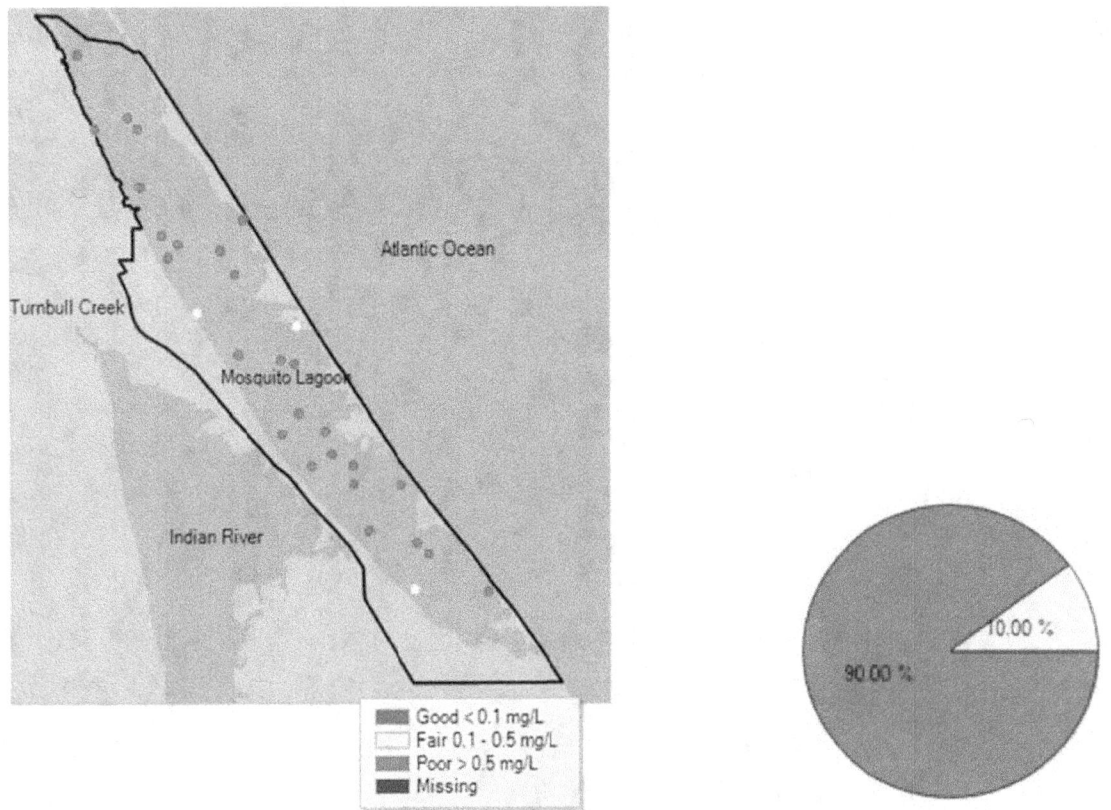

Good < 0.1 mg/L
Fair 0.1 - 0.5 mg/L
Poor > 0.5 mg/L
Missing

Figure 6. Total dissol ed nitrogen (TDN) concentrations at C anaveral National Seashore in July 2009. Graph shows percent ige of sites in each condition category.

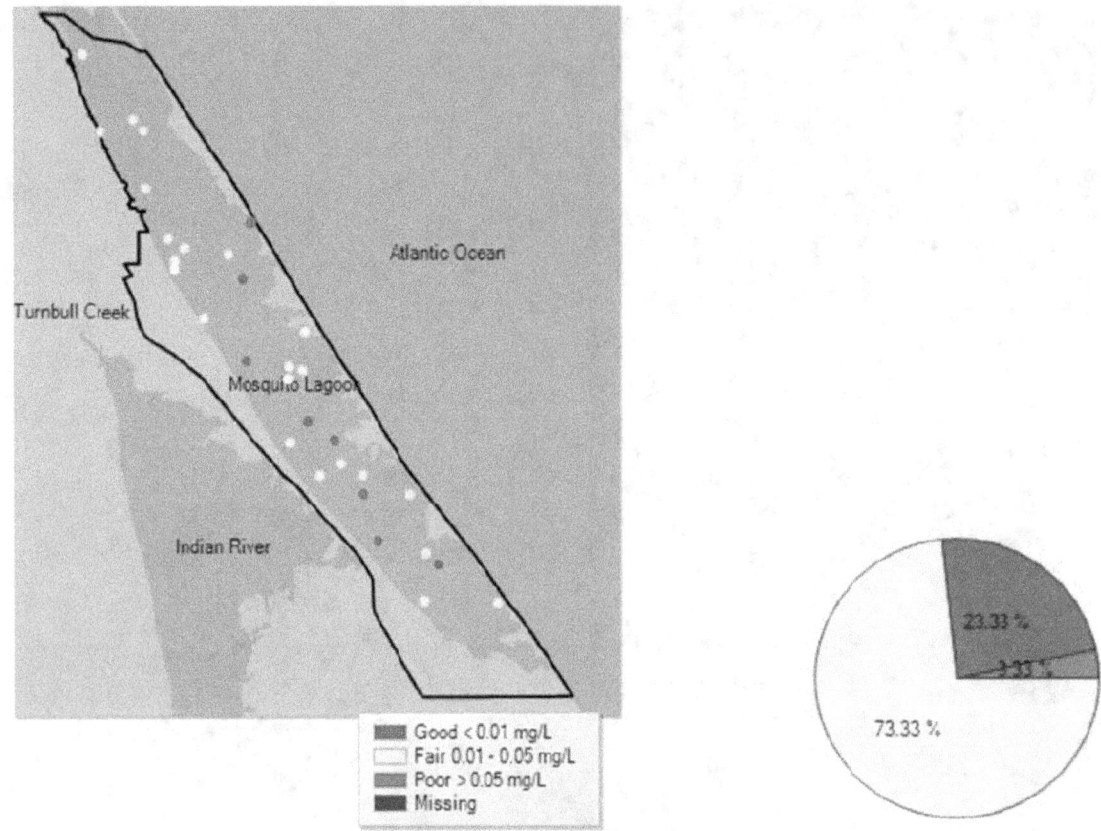

Figure 7. Total dissol ed phosphorus (TDP) concentrations at Canaveral National Seashore during July 2009. Gr ph shows p rcentage of sites in each condition cat gory.

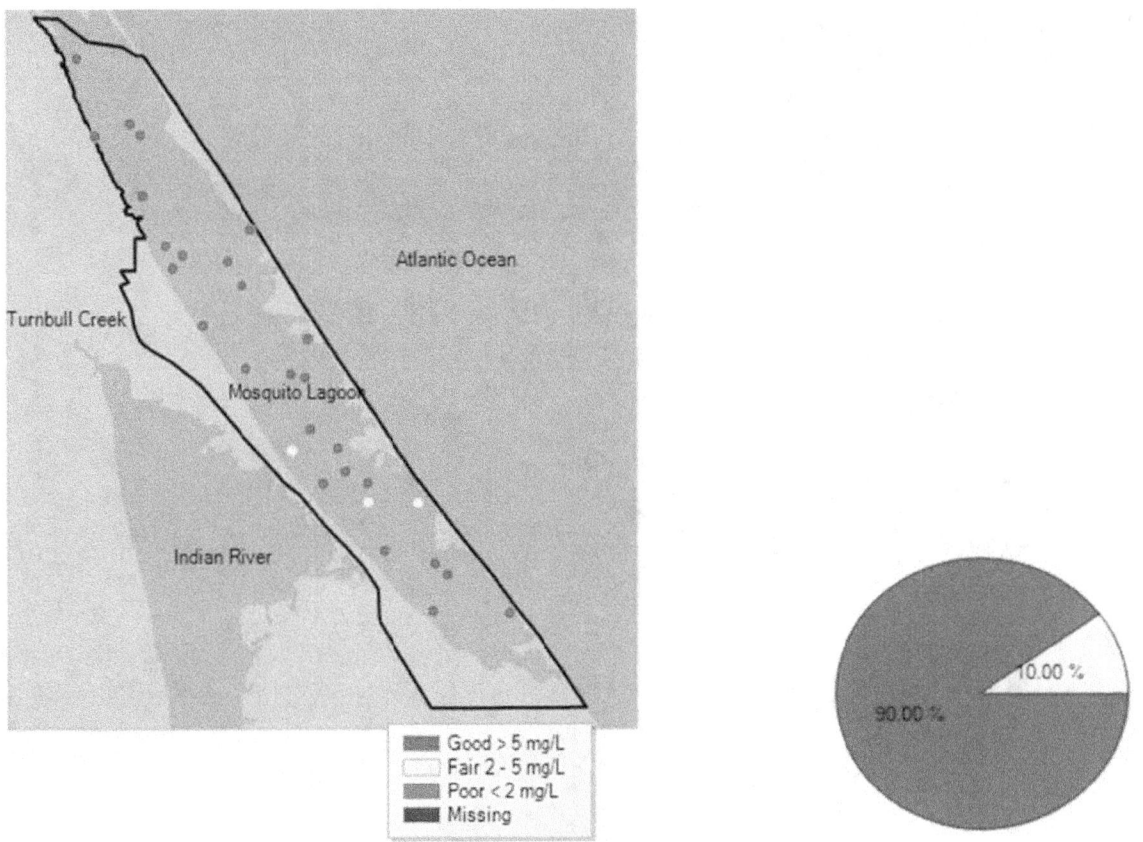

Figure 8. Dissolved oxygen concentrations at Canaveral Na ional Seash re in July 2009. Graph shows percenta ɟe of sites in each condition category.

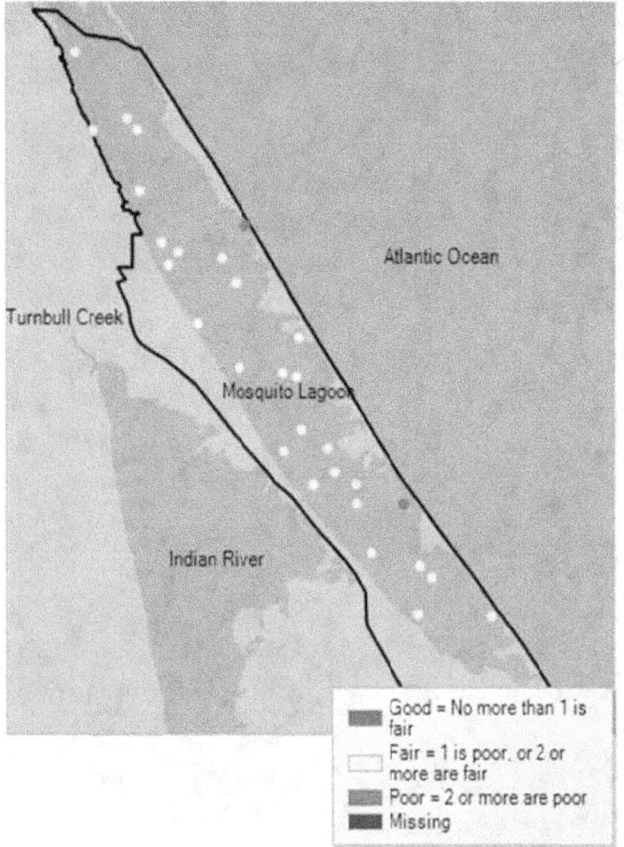

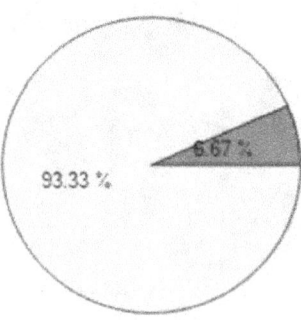

Figure 9. Park wide water-quality conditions at Canaveral National Seashore during July 2009. Assessment based on numbers of categorical ratings at each site for using the water clarity index (K), chlorophyll a, total dissolved nitrogen, total dissolved phosphorus and dissolved oxygen measurements. Graph shows percentage of sites in each condition category.

Sedi ient Condition Assessments

Figures 0, 11, and 2 are maps which show the spatial distribution of sampling sites and the corresponding ratings for sediment contamination based on a summary of data collected at each site. Inset graphs on each figure show the percentage of sites in eac rating category. Data used to make maps and g aphs are found in tables 6, 7, and 8.

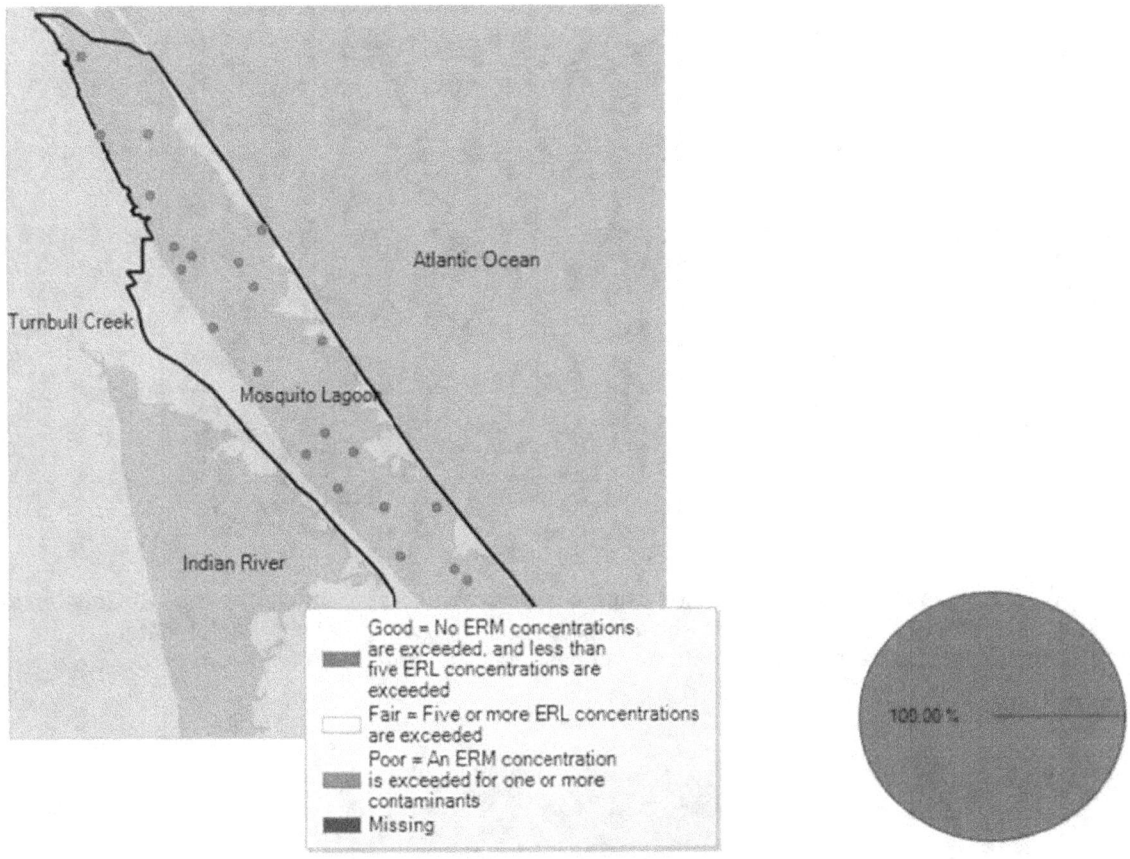

Figure 1). Sediment ontaminant rating at Canaveral Nation al Seashore in July 2009. Assessment categories correspond to numbers of ERM and ERL concentrations exceeded at a site. Inset graph shows percentage of ites in each condition category.

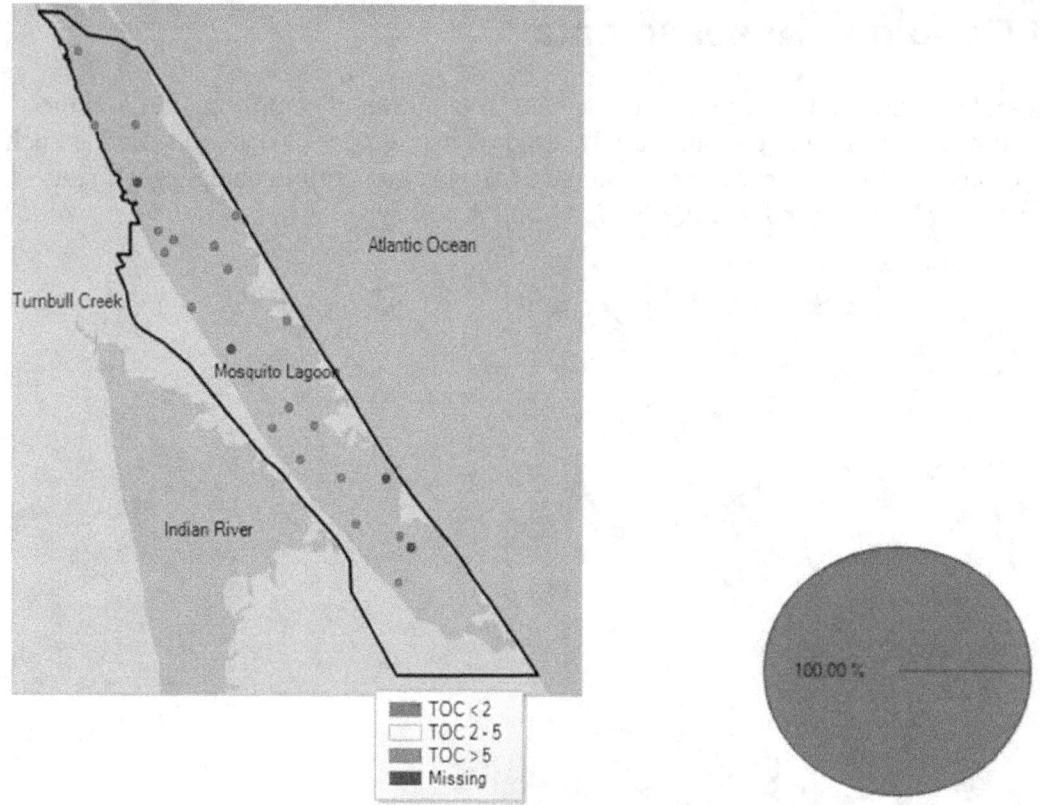

Figure 1 I. Total Orga ic Carbon (TOC) concentrations in se iments and condition ratings at Canaveral National Seashore in July 2009. Inset graph shows percenta e of sites in each condition category. Estimate I values wer used at sites were data were missing. All estimate I values were below 2 percent.

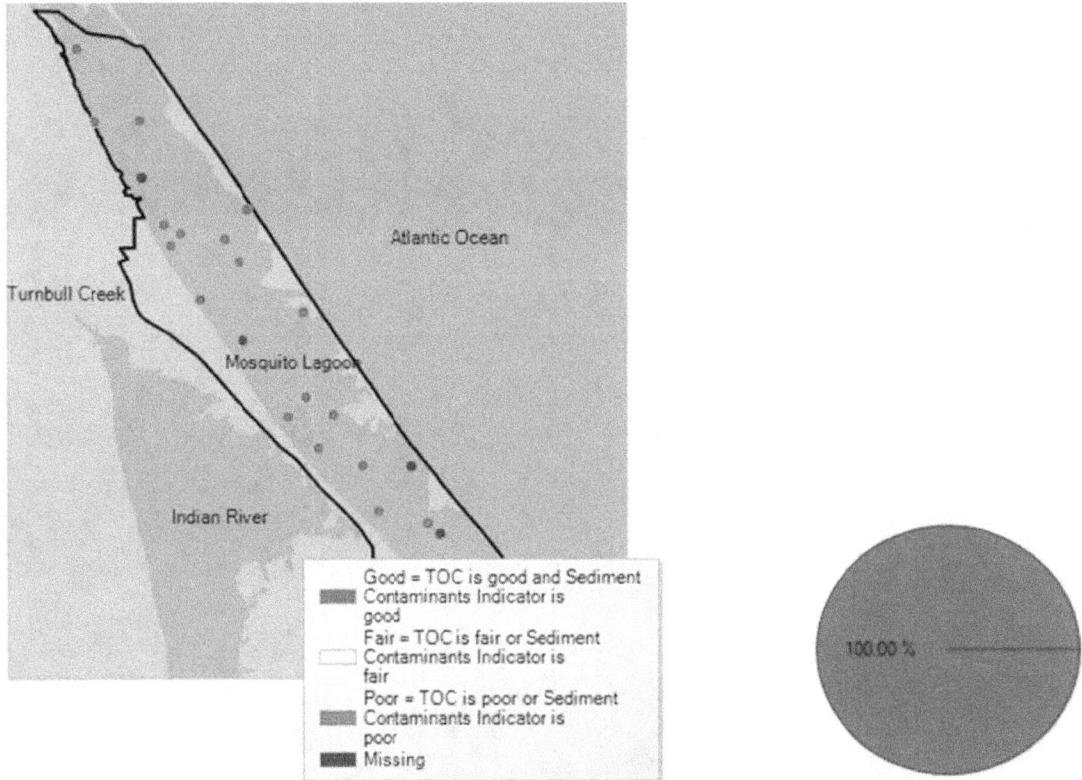

Figure 2. Sediment quality index ratings at Canaveral National Seashore in July 2009. Inset graph shows percentage of sites in each condition category. Estimated values were used at blue sites.

Water-Quality Data

Table 5. Water-quality parameter values and assessment conditions for sites sampled at Canaveral National Seashore in July 2009 Water Clarity Index (*k*) values were calculated using constant for estuarine water with naturally turbid conditions (Smith et al., 2006). Condition of assessed parameter from USEPA (2005). [Green, *good*; yellow, *fair;* and red, *poor*; blue, missing data; *k*, light attenuation coefficient; ug/L, micrograms per liter; mg/l, milligrams per liter]

Station	Water Clarity Index (WCI)	Chlorophyll a (ug/L)	Total Dissolved Nitrogen (mg/L)	Total Dissolved Phosphorus (mg/L)	Dissolved Oxygen (mg/L)
CANA-01	1.563	9.850	0.870	0.013	5.990
CANA-02	1.266	5.450	0.896	0.011	5.340
CANA-03	1.266	10.250	0.946	0.007	4.310
CANA-04	1.266	3.600	0.948	0.011	7.250
CANA-05	1.031	5.250	0.916	0.010	5.820
CANA-06		2.000	0.928	0.010	8.560
CANA-07	1.205	11.100	0.790	0.015	5.620
CANA-08	0.943	4.950	0.866	0.008	5.810
CANA-09	2.381	16.450	0.702	0.011	7.400
CANA-10		1.950	0.988	0.009	10.880
CANA-11	1.667	14.850	0.775	0.013	4.870
CANA-12	3.030	3.650	1.020	0.010	3.910
CANA-13	1.563	8.000	0.919	0.013	6.740
CANA-14		5.950	0.454	0.015	7.790
CANA-15	1.429	10.800	0.742	0.015	8.640
CANA-17	1.316	5.850	0.664	0.011	6.040
CANA-18		1.200	0.606	0.010	8.720
CANA-19		3.350	0.543	0.009	9.730
CANA-20		4.300	0.491	0.010	9.940
CANA-21	2.857	8.600	0.590	0.012	13.050
CANA-23	1.754	8.950	0.676	0.008	7.080
CANA-24		1.300	0.709	0.016	13.830
CANA-25	2.000	6.250	0.695	0.158	8.360
CANA-27	5.556	6.800	0.442	0.014	9.100
CANA-29	1.515	12.800	0.808	0.027	5.120
CANA-ALT-01	1.786	8.250	0.500	0.015	5.200
CANA-ALT-02	1.136	2.500	0.900	0.007	6.690
CANA-ALT-03	1.538	5.450	0.642	0.019	6.600
CANA-ALT-04	1.449	2.650	0.752	0.009	6.520
CANA-ALT-05		4.500	1.098	0.010	9.500

Sediment-Quality Data

Table 6. Concentrations of select metals (in ppm) for sites sampled at Canaveral National Seashore during July 2009. Condition of assessed constituent from Long et al. (1995). [Green, *good*; yellow, *fair*; red, *poor*; —, value not reported, below the detection limit; *, estimated value, used in condition assessment summaries]

Station	Arsenic	Cadmium	Chromium	Copper	Lead	Mercury	Nickel	Silver	Zinc
CANA-01	-	*0.15	5.5	*0.68	5.1	-	*0.84	-	*2.4
CANA-02	-	*0.21	8.5	*1.6	8.3	*0.017	*1.8	-	*5.5
CANA-03	-	*0.18	7.3	*1.4	6.8	*0.016	*1.5	-	*4.3
CANA-04	-	*0.16	*4.0	*0.91	5.2	*0.021	*0.72	-	*1.6
CANA-05	*1.3	-	11.8	*3.0	5.5	0.034	*2.0	*0.064	*9.9
CANA-07	*1.6	*0.15	11.2	*4.3	5.9	*0.022	*2.3	*0.045	*7.9
CANA-08	*1.1	*0.16	7.5	*1.1	5.2	*0.017	*1.6	-	*4.9
CANA-09	*1.5	*0.21	13.5	*2.1	10.8	*0.016	*2.9	-	*9.2
CANA-10	-	*0.19	6.9	*1.1	7.0	*0.013	*1.6	-	*3.5
CANA-11	-	*0.16	*4.6	*0.73	4.7	*0.013	*1.0	-	*2.1
CANA-12	-	*0.16	*4.1	*1.0	5.1	*0.012	*0.7	-	*2.2
CANA-13	-	*0.12	*2.9	*1.6	3.2	*0.015	*0.46	-	-
CANA-14	*3.5	*0.2	16.9	*3.2	9.3	*0.03	*3.8	0.043	10.6
CANA-15	-	*0.18	5.2	*1.5	4.2	*0.019	*1.1	-	*3.3
CANA-17	-	*0.17	*4.5	*0.8	5.8	*0.019	*0.75	-	*1.6
CANA-19	-	*0.17	*3.3	*0.8	4.0	*0.015	*0.52	-	*1.0
CANA-20	-	*0.12	*2.4	*0.67	2.2	*0.012	-	-	*2.6
CANA-23	-	-	-	-	-	*0.02	-	-	*2.8
CANA-25	-	*0.14	*1.3	*0.64	2.3	*0.012	*0.35	-	-
CANA-27	-	*0.17	*3.8	*0.58	7.0	*0.0091	*0.64	-	*0.86
CANA-29	-	*0.2	*4.7	*0.7	4.7	*0.013	*0.89	-	*2.1
CANA-ALT-02	*3.0	*0.26	18.1	*2.7	10.3	0.05	*3.9	0.054	13.1
CANA-ALT-03	-	*0.14	*3.7	*0.73	4.8	*0.011	*0.62	-	*1.2
CANA-ALT-04	*3.1	*0.27	27.1	*4.9	11.8	0.04	6.0	*0.06	22.1

Table 7. Organic contaminant concentrations (in ppb) and totals for select classes of compounds for sites sampled at Canaveral National Seashore during July, 2009. [Green, good; yellow, fair; red, poor; —, value not reported, below the detection limit]

Station	2-Methylnaphthalene	4,4'-DDE	Acenaphthene	Acenaphthylene	Anthracene	Benz[a]anthracene	Benzo[a]pyrene	Chrysene	Dibenz[a,h]anthracene	Fluoranthene	Fluorene	Naphthalene	Phenanthrene	Pyrene	Total DDT	High molecular weight PAH	Low molecular weight PAH	Total PAHs	Total PCBs
CANA-01	-	-	-	-	-	-	-	-	-	-	-	-	-	-	0	0	0	0	0
CANA-02	-	-	-	-	-	-	-	-	-	-	-	-	-	-	0	0	0	0	0
CANA-03	-	-	-	-	-	-	-	-	-	-	-	-	-	-	0	0	0	0	0
CANA-04	-	-	-	-	-	-	-	-	-	-	-	-	-	-	0	0	0	0	0
CANA-05	-	-	-	-	-	-	-	-	-	-	-	-	-	-	0	0	0	0	0
CANA-07	-	-	-	-	-	-	-	-	-	-	-	-	-	-	0	0	0	0	0
CANA-08	-	-	-	-	-	-	-	-	-	-	-	-	-	-	0	0	0	0	0
CANA-09	-	-	-	-	-	-	-	-	-	-	-	-	-	-	0	0	0	0	0
CANA-10	-	-	-	-	-	-	-	-	-	-	-	-	-	-	0	0	0	0	0
CANA-11	-	-	-	-	-	-	-	-	-	-	-	-	-	-	0	0	0	0	0
CANA-12	-	-	-	-	-	-	-	-	-	-	-	-	-	-	0	0	0	0	0
CANA-13	-	-	-	-	-	-	-	-	-	-	-	-	-	-	0	0	0	0	0
CANA-14	-	-	-	-	-	-	-	-	-	-	-	-	-	-	0	0	0	0	0
CANA-15	-	-	-	-	-	-	-	-	-	-	-	-	-	-	0	0	0	0	0
CANA-17	-	-	-	-	-	-	-	-	-	-	-	-	-	-	0	0	0	0	0
CANA-19	-	-	-	-	-	-	-	-	-	-	-	-	-	-	0	0	0	0	0
CANA-20	-	-	-	-	-	-	-	-	-	-	-	-	-	-	0	0	0	0	0
CANA-23	-	-	-	-	-	-	-	-	-	-	-	-	-	-	0	0	0	0	0
CANA-25	-	-	-	-	-	-	-	-	-	-	-	-	-	-	0	0	0	0	0
CANA-27	-	-	-	-	-	-	-	-	-	-	-	-	-	-	0	0	0	0	0
CANA-29	-	-	-	-	-	-	-	-	-	-	-	-	-	-	0	0	0	0	0
CANA-ALT-02	-	-	-	-	-	-	-	-	-	-	-	-	-	-	0	0	0	0	0
CANA-ALT-03	-	-	-	-	-	-	-	-	-	-	-	-	-	-	0	0	0	0	0
CANA-ALT-04	-	-	-	-	-	-	-	-	-	-	-	-	-	-	0	0	0	0	0

Table 8. Sediment contaminant rating, total organic carbon (TOC), and Sediment Quality Index (SQI) rating for sites sampled Canaveral National Seashore during July 2009. [Green, *good*; yellow, *fair*; red, *poor*; blue, missing data; **, values estimated using relation between percent sand and TOC concentration established by regression]

Station	Sediment Contaminant Rating	Total Organic Carbon (%)	Sediment Quality Index
CANA-01	Good	0.0323	Good
CANA-02	Good	0.0817	Good
CANA-03	Good	0.106	Good
CANA-04	Good	0.0806	Good
CANA-05	Good	0.0808	Good
CANA-07	Good	0.112	Good
CANA-08	Good	0.0977	Good
CANA-09	Good	0.112	Good
CANA-10	Good	0.0827	Good
CANA-11	Good	0.0636	Good
CANA-12	Good	0.0463**	Good**
CANA-13	Good	0.0264	Good
CANA-14	Good	0.0757	Good
CANA-15	Good	0.033	Good
CANA-17	Good	0.0248	Good
CANA-19	Good	0.0365	Good
CANA-20	Good	0.0406	Good
CANA-23	Good	0.0718	Good
CANA-25	Good	0.0241	Good
CANA-27	Good	0.0187	Good
CANA-29	Good	0.0328	Good
CANA-ALT-02	Good	0.1261**	Good**
CANA-ALT-03	Good	0.0433**	Good**
CANA-ALT-04	Good	0.0884**	Good**

Literature Cited

DeVivo, J. C., C. J. Wright, M. W. Byrne, E. DiDonato, and T. Curtis. 2008. Vital signs monitoring in the Southeast Coast Inventory & Monitoring Network. Natural Resource Report NPS/SECN/NRR—2008/061. National Park Service, Fort Collins, Colorado.

DeVivo, J. C., E. M. DiDonato, C. J.Wright, Y. Li, and M. B. Gregory, Assessment of estuarine water and sediment quality in the Southeast Coast Network, *in review*.

Holland, A. F., D. M. Sanger, C. P. Gawle, S. B. Lerberg, M. S. Santiago, G. H. M. Riekerk, L. E. Zimmerman, and G. I. Scott. 2004. Linkages between tidal creek ecosystems and the landscape and demographic attributes of their wetlands. Journal of Experimental Marine Biology and Ecology 298: 151-178.

Lerberg, S. B., A. F. Holland, and D. Sanger. 2000. Responses of tidal creek macrobenthic communities to the effects of watershed development. Estuaries 23(6): 838-853.

Long, E. R., D. D. MacDonald, S. L. Smith, and F. D. Calder. 1995. Incidence of adverse biological effects within ranges of chemical concentrations in marine and estuarine sediments. Environmental Management 19(1): 81–97.

Smith, L. M. V. D. Engle, and J. K. Summers. 2006. Assessing water clarity as a component of water quality in the Gulf of Mexico estuaries. Environmental Monitoring and Assessment. 115:291-305.

Stevens, D. L., Jr. 1997. Variable density grid-based sampling designs for continuous spatial populations. Envirometrics 8: 167-195.

Stevens, D. L., Jr. and A. R. Olsen. 1999. Spatially restricted surveys over time for aquatic resources. Journal of Agricultural, Biological and Environmental Statistics 4: 415-428.

Stevens, D. and A. R. Olsen. 2004. Spatially balanced sampling of natural resources. Journal of the American Statistical Association 99: 262-278.

U.S. EPA. 2001. Environmental Monitoring an Assessment Program (EMAP). National Coastal Assessment Quality Assurance Project Plan 2001 – 2004. United States Environmental Protection Agency, Office of Research and Development, National Health and Environmental Effects Research Laboratory, gulf Ecology Division, gulf Breeze, FL. EPA/620/R-01/002.

U.S. EPA. 2005. National Coastal Condition Report II. EPA-620/R-03/002. Office of Research and Development and Office of Water, Washington, D.C., USA.